W9-CEE-376

MANAGING DISAGREEMENT CONSTRUCTIVELY

Revised Edition

Conflict Management in Organizations

Herbert S. Kindler, Ph.D.

A FIFTY-MINUTE™ SERIES BOOK

CRISP PUBLICATIONS, INC.
Menlo Park, California

MANAGING DISAGREEMENT CONSTRUCTIVELY

CONFLICT MANAGEMENT IN ORGANIZATIONS

Revised Edition

Herbert S. Kindler, Ph.D.

CREDITS
Managing Editor: **Kathleen Barcos**
Editor: **Kay Keppler**
Typesetting: **ExecuStaff**
Cover Design: **Carol Harris**
Artwork: **Ralph Mapson**

All rights reserved. No part of this book may be reproduced or transmitted in any form or by any means now known or to be invented, electronic or mechanical, including photocopying, recording, or by any information storage or retrieval system without written permission from the author or publisher, except for the brief inclusion of quotations in a review.

© 1996 Crisp Publications, Inc.
Printed in the United States of America by Bawden Printing Company.

http://www.crisp-pub.com

Distribution to the U.S. Trade:

National Book Network, Inc.
4720 Boston Way
Lanham, MD 20706
1-800-462-6420

Library of Congress Catalog Card Number 95-83683
Kindler, Herbert S.
Managing Disagreement Constructively–Revised
ISBN 1-56052-383-2

98 99 00 01   10 9 8 7 6 5 4 3 2

This book is printed on recyclable paper with soy ink.

Learning Objectives for:

MANAGING DISAGREEMENT CONSTRUCTIVELY

The objectives for *Managing Disagreement Constructively—Revised Edition* are listed below. They have been developed to guide you, the reader, to the core issues covered in this book.

Objectives

❑ **1) To present basic principles of managing conflict**

❑ **2) To point out inappropriate procedures in managing disagreement**

❑ **3) To point out strategies that may work in managing disagreement**

Assessing Your Progress

In addition to the learning objectives, Crisp, Inc. has developed an **assessment** that covers the fundamental information presented in this book. A twenty-five item, multiple choice/true-false questionnaire allows the reader to evaluate his or her comprehension of the subject matter. An answer sheet with a chart matching the questions to the listed objectives is also available. To learn how to obtain a copy of this assessment please call: **1-800-442-7477** and ask to speak with a Customer Service Representative.

Assessments should not be used in any selection process.

ABOUT THE AUTHOR

Herbert S. Kindler, Ph.D., developed the material for this book in the course of providing training programs on managing conflict and disagreement for IBM, General Motors, ARCO, Hughes Aircraft Company, American Association of Retired Persons, City of Santa Barbara, TRW, Purdue University Hospitals, JVC, U.S. Navy, Mercedes Benz, UCLA, Navistar, and Starbucks among others.

His 25 years of experience in a variety of positions include chief executive officer. Dr. Kindler graduated from M.I.T. and received his doctorate in management from UCLA.

As director of the Center for Management Effectiveness, he provides consulting and training services. Dr. Kindler conducts management seminars in the United States and abroad and is listed in *Who's Who in America*.

He welcomes comments from readers and can be reached by writing Center for Management Effectiveness, P.O. Box 1202, Pacific Palisades, CA 90272 or phoning (310) 459-6052.

CONTENTS

> "Contact is the Appreciation
> of Differences."
>
> —Fritz Perls

PREFACE

The constructive handling of disagreement is central to personal satisfaction and organizational effectiveness. Improved skills in managing interpersonal differences will enrich your work, your relationships and your career.

This book will help you:

- anticipate and prevent destructive conflict

- deal with disagreement before it erupts out of control

- use differences as a springboard to creative problem seeking and solving

- manage disagreement with more skill and assurance

This revised edition reflects feedback received from trainers who used the book in their workshops on conflict management, leadership training, interpersonal communication, and managing diversity.

Several exercises, which help readers "learn from doing" as well as from reading, have been expanded. As you read through the book, you frequently will be invited to complete these clarifying exercises.

The structure of this book—and the structure of training programs based on the book—has three basic components:

- **Guiding Principles**

- **Nine Approaches to Managing Disagreement**

- **Four-Phase Process**

Rather than pat prescriptions, possibilities are suggested that apply in practical, everyday situations—both at work and in your personal life.

Herb Kindler

Herbert S. Kindler, Ph.D.

INTRODUCTION

Disagreement among people in relationships, groups, and organizations comes with the territory. It's common to hear:

> "What I dislike most about disagreement is the endless arguing and having to listen to someone else's stored-up anger and resentment. Who needs it?"
>
> "We could be doing something a lot more productive than dancing around our differences. It's a waste of time because people don't really change their minds anyway."
>
> "Sure, I could be understanding and listen to why a worker doesn't want to follow my instructions. But all I'm going to get for my trouble is that others will start questioning what I say and I'll be seen by my boss as a weak manager. As far as I'm concerned, nice guys finish last."

Every encounter with someone whose views differ from our own offers the potential for friction, wasted time, bruised feelings, and looking foolish.

Managing interpersonal differences isn't easy. Signs of mismanagement are everywhere—back-biting rivalry, bitter divorces, bickering co-workers. Mishandling these differences leaves emotional scars, diverts energy from where it's really needed and undermines morale. No wonder so many people walk away from disagreement. Despite the risk of pain and irritation, the rewards for handling disagreement constructively are gratifying.

INTRODUCTION (continued)

Take a few moments now to consider what *specific benefits you* would gain from sharpening your conflict management skills. Think about situations both at work and in your home life. Write the major benefits below.

_____

_____

_____

_____

_____

Check your list against the following benefits that others report they've experienced after managing disagreement effectively. Their feedback may suggest points you overlooked.

1. "I cleared up misunderstandings with my boss (son, wife, neighbor, friend, etc.)."

2. "I let go of old resentments and started building a more cooperative relationship."

3. "Creative ideas came out of our meeting that were a lot better than the approach I had been pushing for."

4. "Problems surfaced that I didn't even suspect existed."

5. "Teamwork improved because we started to feel more trust in one another—and more mutual respect."

6. "I felt more committed to the decision we agreed on."

When you succeed in managing disagreement constructively, everyone wins. The stage is set for needed change, clearer communication, creative ideas, and more authentic relationships.

SECTION

I

Understanding Conflict
Management

GUIDING PRINCIPLES

As you review the concepts and techniques for managing disagreement presented in this book, keep in mind the underlying values. Their essence—embodied in these principles—is to honor the legitimate interests of all involved persons.

1. Preserve Dignity and Respect

Preserve and protect the dignity of all *stakeholders* (shorthand for "people who have an important stake in issues under consideration"), including your own. In a heated discussion, it's easy to say something demeaning. Keep your focus on issues, not personalities.

Until proved otherwise, assume the other person is expressing a legitimate concern when disagreeing. Even if someone who disagrees with you appears stubborn or stupid, you won't get closer to resolving a dispute by putting them down.

When you show sincere respect for people who disagree with you, they will be less inclined to be defensive. You can avoid those energy-draining, win-lose battles that are really about saving face.

2. Listen with Empathy—Be Fully Present*

When you listen to others' views, put yourself in their shoes. See from their perspective; feel the speaker's emotional state. When ideas conflict with what you already believe, notice if you discount the speaker's message. To get the full information that is basic to managing differences, you need to listen with a neutrality that suspends critical judgment.

When you listen with full presence, you convey the message: "I respect you as a person. Your thoughts and feelings are important to me whether or not I agree with them."

Give your full attention to appreciating how come the other person sees the same situation differently from you. Be receptive to more than the words you hear—they always carry more meaning than their explicit content. When the other person feels "heard," you will have taken an important, though subtle, step toward resolving your disagreement.

*An excellent book on this topic is *The Business of Listening* by Diane Bone, Crisp Publications.

GUIDING PRINCIPLES (continued)

3. Find Common Ground Without Forcing Change

Overarching mutual concern and interest paves the way to move from disagreement to win-win resolution. The only disagreements of any real importance are those that involve people in *interdependent relationships—where each person d*epends on the other to get a task done or to gain satisfaction. Therefore, inherent in mutual dependence is the existence of common ground.

In a dispute, it is tempting to force or expect others to change their basic orientation or behavioral style. People, oneself included, change basic patterns only with difficulty, only where there is trust, and only when they believe it is in their best interest to change. Until trust and respect are established, what helps is a shared larger vision and common long-range goals.

4. Honor Diversity, Including Your Own Perspective

Different viewpoints spur the creative search for resolution. In contrast, when people converge quickly and reach instant agreement, the process is sterile. Nothing new has been added.

When you're the lone dissenter, it's tempting to surrender your conviction to conform with more popular views. Your *gift* to others is your independent point of view—which requires that you understand what really matters to *you*. Diversity holds the seeds for constructive change.

These guidelines—preserving dignity and respect, listening for the message even when you don't agree with it, seeking common ground, and honoring diversity—comprise an attitudinal framework helpful in resolving disagreement. With these principles, you communicate, "I honor you and your needs. I take responsibility for letting you know my views. We can manage our differences constructively."

WHAT'S YOUR STYLE?

On the following pages is an assessment you can take to evaluate your own conflict resolution style. On the scoring sheet on page 10 are the nine approaches to conflict management. When you have completed the *MODI-Self* exercise and computed your scores, you can explore further your results using information provided immediately after the exercise.

NOTE: Additional copies of *MODI-Self*, starting on page 6, may be ordered by using the address on the bottom of the following page. Each MODI-Self booklet is 12 pages with a full-color cover appropriate for personal use and training programs.

You may also order copies of *MODI-Feedback so* that you can ask others at home or with whom you work for their perceptions. *MODI-Feedback* scores provide you with information on *how others see you* managing disagreement with them. Where *MODI-Self and MODI-Feedback* scores diverge by 3 or more points, you may want to discuss ways to bring your perceptions into closer alignment.

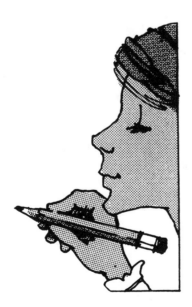

SELF-ASSESSMENT EXERCISE: MODI-Self™
Management Of Differences Inventory™

Directions

On the following pages are pairs of statements that describe alternative ways of responding to situations involving differing views.

When you deal with differences with others, you may respond one way at one time and another way at another time depending on the situation and who is involved. The Inventory takes this into account by providing for you to distribute 3 points between two statements—to show how frequently you relate to others in each of the two ways indicated.

If you respond very differently with different people, you may complete a MODI-Self Inventory for each person with whom you frequently interact.

Focus your answers on how you actually behave rather than on how you might like to behave. There are no right or wrong answers.

For each pair of statements that follow, allocate *exactly 3 points* between the alternatives to show how frequently you behave as described, using these guidelines:

3 = very often,   2 = moderately often,   1 = occasionally,   0 = rarely or never

Use only whole numbers, not fractions.

EXAMPLE

In a disagreement, dispute, or difference or view with another:

0. a. ③ I set out to win the argument.   **a.** ② **a.** ① **a.** ⓪
                                           OR   **OR**   **OR**
b. ⓪ I withdraw to check my facts.   **b.** ① **b.** ② **b.** ③

Each pair of scores must add up to 3 exactly.

© Copyright 1981, Revised 1994 by Center for Management Effectiveness. All rights reserved. May not be reproduced in any form without permission of the Center, P.O. Box 1202, Pacific Palisades, CA 90272.

Scoring: 3 = Very often, 2 = Moderately often, 1 = Occasionally, 0 = Rarely
IN A DISAGREEMENT, DISPUTE, OR DIFFERENCE OF VIEW WITH ANOTHER:

1. a. ☐ I let emotions and tensions cool before taking decisive action.
b. ☐ We find some formula or other criteria we both agree on.

2. a. ☐ I assert myself to gain what I'm after.
b. ☐ We jointly develop a mutually agreeable plan that merges both views.

3. a. ☐ I follow my view, and the other person follows his or her view.
b. ☐ I give in on some points to get my way on others.

4. a. ☐ I place more emphasis on similarities and less emphasis on differences.
b. ☐ We find logical rules we both agree on as the basis for our decision.

5. a. ☐ We take action that lets both parties retain their positions, at least on an interim basis.
b. ☐ Within agreed-upon limits, I give control to the other person.

6. a. ☐ I gain agreement for my position by avoiding details on which we may disagree.
b. ☐ I try solutions proposed by the other person.

7. a. ☐ I push to have my approach or my ideas prevail.
b. ☐ I go along with the other person's view.

8. a. ☐ We work out a fair combination of gains and losses for both of us.
b. ☐ I get both our concerns out in the open, and we problem-solve together.

9. a. ☐ I wait until I feel better prepared to take action.
b. ☐ I let the other person come up with the plan.

10. a. ☐ I avoid unnecessary problems by delaying action.
b. ☐ We agree to disagree, at least for a while or on an experimental basis.

11. a. ☐ I sell the person who disagrees with me on accepting my view by emphasizing its positive features.
b. ☐ I fully express my ideas and feelings, and urge the other person to do the same.

12. a. ☐ We find some formula to resolve our differences.
b. ☐ We find solutions in which gains balance out losses for both parties.

13. a. ☐ I do what it takes to get my ideas accepted.
b. ☐ I allow the other person, within limits, to resolve our issue.

Making copies of this material by any method is a violation of copyright law.

Scoring: **3 = Very often, 2 = Moderately often, 1 = Occasionally, 0 = Rarely**	
IN A DISAGREEMENT, DISPUTE, OR DIFFERENCE OF VIEW WITH ANOTHER:	

14. a. ☐ We mutually agree on rules or procedures to resolve our differences.

  b. ☐ I accommodate myself to the other person's view.

15. a. ☐ I gain compliance to my views.

  b. ☐ We acknowledge and allow each other's differences.

16. a. ☐ I go along with the views of the other person.

  b. ☐ We work together to integrate ideas of both persons.

17. a. ☐ I minimize presenting information that makes my position less attractive.

  b. ☐ Within a given framework, I let the other person handle the issue.

18. a. ☐ I wait until I have more information or emotions cool.

  b. ☐ We find a mutually acceptable compromise by which to resolve our differences.

19. a. ☐ I delay suggesting changes until the timing feels right.

  b. ☐ I don't resist the views of the other person.

20. a. ☐ We find mutually agreeable procedures (such as taking a vote or an appropriate test).

  b. ☐ We find ways to jointly reframe our differences to satisfy both our needs.

21. a. ☐ I give in on some points if I believe the other person will reciprocate.

  b. ☐ I state my expectations and concerns and let the other person work out a solution.

22. a. ☐ I show the other person that in the final analysis our views aren't very different.

  b. ☐ I give the other person a turn or concession if I believe he or she will do the same for me.

23. a. ☐ We find ways that allow each of us to pursue our individual viewpoints.

  b. ☐ We find solutions that take both our views into account.

24. a. ☐ I deal with differences only after waiting until I feel the time is right.

  b. ☐ I act in ways that advance my position.

Making copies of this material by any method is a violation of copyright law.

Scoring: 3 = Very often,   2 = Moderately often,   1 = Occasionally,   0 = Rarely
IN A DISAGREEMENT, DISPUTE, OR DIFFERENCE OF VIEW WITH ANOTHER:

25. a. ☐ We mutually agree on a rule or procedure that will decide the issue.
   b. ☐ We find ways in which we can both pursue our respective points of view.

26. a. ☐ I yield to the other person's views.
   b. ☐ Given acceptable boundaries, I am willing to have the other person handle the issue.

27. a. ☐ I prevail on the other person to change his or her mind.
   b. ☐ I establish an objective basis with the other person for resolving our differences.

28. a. ☐ I put off dealing with our differences until I have enough information.
   b. ☐ I resolve our differences by emphasizing where we are not so far apart in our thinking.

29. a. ☐ We settle our differences by working out a compromise solution.
   b. ☐ I accommodate myself to the other person's approach.

30. a. ☐ I point out that our differences aren't substantial enough to argue over.
   b. ☐ I oppose the other person's view.

31. a. ☐ I defer making changes until I have adequate support.
   b. ☐ We find new perspectives that satisfy both our needs.

32. a. ☐ I express some, but not all the negative aspects of my position.
   b. ☐ I get agreement from the other person to live with our differences, at least for a period of time.

33. a. ☐ We jointly agree to accept a criterion or the decision of a third party as the basis for resolving our differences.
   b. ☐ Within stated bounds, I encourage the other person to take the initiative.

34. a. ☐ I play to win.
   b. ☐ I make adjustments when the other person is willing to do the same.

35. a. ☐ I urge the other person to take the initiative within defined limits.
   b. ☐ We integrate the ideas expressed by both individuals.

36. a. ☐ We agree to follow our separate paths until joint action seems feasible.
   b. ☐ I go along with the other person's ideas.

Making copies of this material by any method is a violation of copyright law.

Managing Disagreement Constructively

SCORING

For each item on the preceding three pages, enter your score in the space below to determine which approaches are used most and least.

A1 MAINTAIN	A2 SMOOTH	A3 DOMINATE	B1 DECIDE BY RULE	B2 COEXIST	B3 BARGAIN	C1 YIELD	C2 RELEASE	C3 COLLABORATE
1a =			1b =					
		2a =						2b =
				3a =	3b =			
	4a =		4b =					
				5a =			5b =	
	6a =					6b =		
		7a =				7b =		
					8a =			8b =
9a =							9b =	
10a =				10b =				
	11a =							11b =
			12a =		12b =			
		13a =					13b =	
			14a =			14b =		
		15a =		15b =				
						16a =		16b =
	17a =						17b =	
18a =					18b =			
19a =						19b =		
			20a =					20b =
					21a =		21b =	
	22a =				22b =			
				23a =				23b =
24a =		24b =						
			25a =	25b =				
						26a =	26b =	
		27a =	27b =					
28a =	28b =							
					29a =	29b =		
	30a =	30b =						
31a =								31b =
	32a =			32b =				
			33a =				33b =	
		34a =			34b =			
							35a =	35b =
				36a =		36b =		
A1	A2	A3	B1	B2	B3	C1	C2	C3

TOTAL

Add the numbers in each column and insert totals above. The sum of totals must equal 108.

NINE APPROACHES—APPLYING EACH STRATEGICALLY

Just as serious golfers play best with a full set of clubs, you can more effectively handle the sand traps of disagreement with a full set of strategic approaches.

Your MODI scores give you insight into which approaches you currently prefer and which you may neglect. To understand the meaning of your scores fully, however, you need definitions and a general idea of where each approach can be used appropriately.

Let's begin with background information.

> When MODI was developed, executives were interviewed who were regarded by their co-workers as skillful in managing disagreement. They were asked: *When your views on work-related issues differ from the views of others who also are importantly involved, how do you prepare to handle such situations?*
>
> During these interviews, two concerns emerged as themes: "How flexible do I want to be as I express my viewpoint?" and "How involved do I want my interaction to be with others who disagree?"
>
> After the two dimensions—v*iewpoint flexibility* and *interaction intensity*—were identified, a survey of the literature of management, political science, social psychology, negotiation and organizational behavior revealed nine approaches that formed the model shown in *Figure 1* on the following page.

The nine approaches in *Figure 1*, alone and in blends, are the tools available to manage conflict. The labels used to identify each approach are intended to be nonjudgmental—assuming *all* can be used effectively when well executed and well matched to the situation. Keep *Figure 1* accessible because it will serve you well in preparing to handle disagreement.

Following is a definition of each strategic approach and general application guidelines. In the space provided, write one specific example, that you personally have encountered for each of the nine approaches.

NINE APPROACHES—APPLYING EACH STRATEGICALLY (continued)

	Firm ← VIEWPOINT → Flexible		
Involved (INTERACTION)	*"Do it my way."* **DOMINATE** You direct, control or resist.	*"Let's make a deal."* **BARGAIN** You trade, take turns or split the difference.	*"Let's work together."* **COLLABORATE** You problem solve together to reach a win-win resolution.
	"Try it. You'll like it." **SMOOTH** You accentuate similarities and downplay differences.	*"Let's agree to disagree."* **COEXIST** You pursue differences independently.	*"It's yours to do."* **RELEASE** You release control within agreed-upon limits.
Neutral	*"Wait."* **MAINTAIN** You postpone confronting differences.	*"Let's be fair."* **DECIDE BY RULE** Objective rules determine how differences will be handled.	*"I'll go along."* **YIELD** You adapt, accommodate, give in, or agree.

FIGURE 1. Nine Approaches to Managing Disagreement between people or groups with a shared concern

1. MAINTAIN

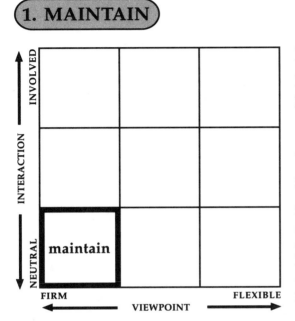

Definition

By delaying or avoiding action, you protect the status quo.

Application

An interim strategy to buy time. Useful when you need to collect information, let emotions cool, enlist allies, deal with higher priorities, allow recent changes to stabilize, or let circumstances resolve the issue (for example, the imminent retirement of an intransigent person).

Example where maintenance is appropriate:

_____

_____

_____

_____

_____

_____

_____

_____

NINE APPROACHES—APPLYING EACH STRATEGICALLY (continued)

2. SMOOTH

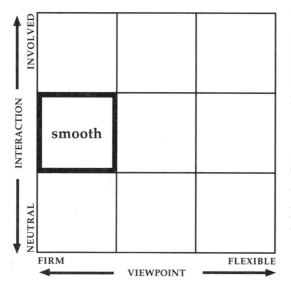

Definition

By focusing exclusively on the benefits of your ideas, without emphasizing (or even mentioning) the alternatives, you sell your ideas.

Application

This form of persuasion is useful when you want your preferences to prevail. It can be used to motivate and as a sales technique.

Example where smoothing is appropriate:

_____

_____

_____

_____

_____

_____

_____

_____

3. DOMINATE

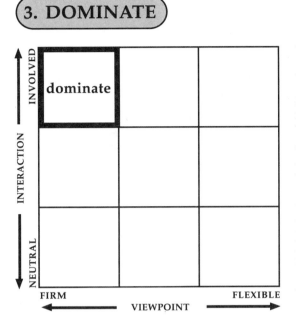

Definition

When the person who holds the greater power insists upon and imposes his or her ideas. This may be accomplished through orders, threats, rewards, penalties and other pressure to gain compliance.

Application

If you possess, or are perceived to possess, authority or power, you may apply this strategy judiciously to ensure physical safety and well-being. Overuse of this approach diminishes its power.

Example where domination is appropriate:

_____

_____

_____

_____

_____

_____

_____

_____

NINE APPROACHES—APPLYING EACH STRATEGICALLY (continued)

4. DECIDE BY RULE

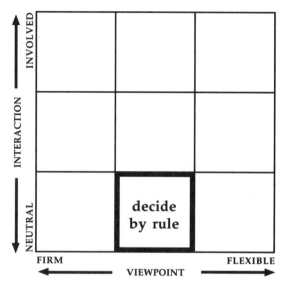

Definition

Joint agreement to use an objective rule or criterion as the basis for choosing among specified alternatives. Examples of deciding by objective rule are lottery, majority rule, seniority, Robert's rules of order, arbitration, a policy ruling, and test scores.

Application

When you want to be impartial and decisive action is needed.

Example where deciding by rule is appropriate:

_____

_____

_____

_____

_____

_____

_____

_____

_____

5. COEXIST

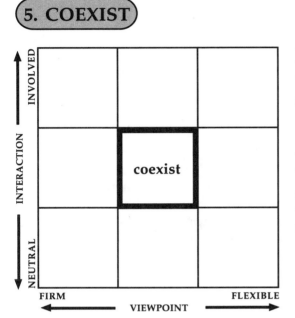

coexist

INVOLVED

INTERACTION

NEUTRAL

FIRM   FLEXIBLE

VIEWPOINT

Definition

When two parties agree to follow separate paths for a period of time.

Application

When two parties of equal power are adamant about the merits of their positions, and no other agreement can be reached.

Example where coexistence is appropriate:

_____

_____

_____

_____

_____

_____

_____

_____

_____

NINE APPROACHES—APPLYING EACH STRATEGICALLY (continued)

6. BARGAIN

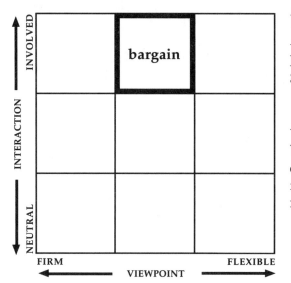

Definition

A mutual agreement in which the parties settle on what should be given or done by each.

Application

When more can be gained from an exchange or by trading (including future reciprocity) than by not reaching any agreement at all.

Example where bargaining is appropriate:

_____

_____

_____

_____

_____

_____

_____

_____

_____

_____

_____

7. YIELD

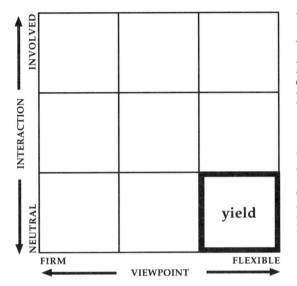

Definition

When you choose to let the other person's point of view prevail and explicitly agree to advance his or her position.

Application

When the issue is important to the other person, but minor to you, or you have more to gain by not resisting.

Example where yielding is appropriate:

_____

_____

_____

_____

_____

_____

_____

_____

_____

NINE APPROACHES—APPLYING EACH STRATEGICALLY (continued)

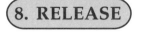

8. RELEASE

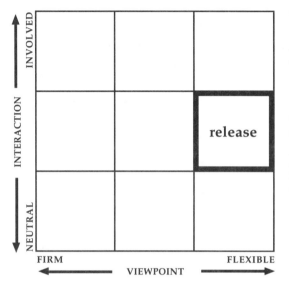

Definition

A giving up of control within limits that are comfortable and appropriate.

Application

When you are in a position of power and there is a low risk of irreversible loss, or an opportunity to encourage another's development.

Example where releasing is appropriate:

_____

_____

_____

_____

_____

_____

_____

_____

_____

_____

_____

9. COLLABORATE

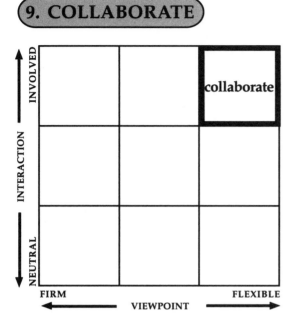

Definition

To work together cooperatively to find a resolution responsive to the concerns of all participants.

Application

When the issues are too important to be compromised and commitment is needed. Useful in team building and strategic decision making. Requires time, trust and inter-personal competence.

Example where collaboration is appropriate:

STYLES TO STRATEGIES

Your effectiveness in dealing with conflict depends on making a deliberate choice of one or more of the just-reviewed nine strategic possibilities. Making your choice consciously requires that you not plunge into a disagreement using a familiar, comfortable, well-worn *style*.

A *style* is a habitual, reactive mode of handling conflict. It is predictable to those who interact with you. A style sometimes fits the situation, sometimes doesn't.

Your aim is to choose *consciously* the approach or combination that works best under each specific circumstance.

In short, your challenge is to convert *styles* to *strategies.* Additional guidance in meeting this challenge is presented in the next section under "Phase II—Plan."

SECTION

II

The Four-Phase Process of Managing Disagreement

FOUR-PHASE PROCESS

As valuable as are *Guiding Principles* and *Strategic Approaches*, you also need a systematic *Process* for dealing with disagreement.

Your process should: (1) anticipate disagreement before it boils over into heated conflict; (2) plan an appropriate strategy; (3) prepare to set your strategy in motion; and (4) take action (or planned inaction), monitoring the results. *Figure 2* presents the framework for this approach, which includes steps to take at each point.

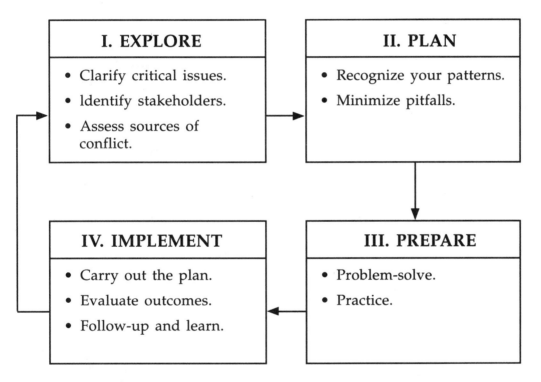

FIGURE 2. Overview of the Managing Disagreement Process

PHASE I: EXPLORE

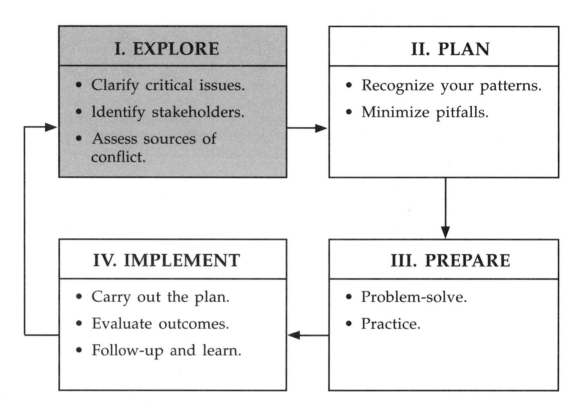

The reasons to explore disagreements in the making are:

► You can listen to others, gather data, develop your views, and determine if opposition is likely.

► You can choose to what extent you want to become personally involved.

► You can select and refine an appropriate strategy, perhaps averting escalation to a full-blown conflict.

At this point, think of a situation where a view you hold is *likely to be opposed* by someone whose agreement or cooperation you need. The setting can be either at work or in your personal life.

If a disagreement doesn't immediately come to mind, focus on a recent or imminent *change* in your organizational or private life. Sometimes change breeds conflict; sometimes conflict begets change. In either event, potential for disagreement is rooted in change.

Because we will be referring back to the situation you describe, please write in a description of a *disagreement that is developing (or has developed) that really matters to you.* Include what led up to the present state of affairs and its current status.

Description of your current (or potential) disagreement.

_____

_____

_____

_____

_____

_____

_____

_____

_____

_____

_____

_____

Following is a real-life case that provides another frame of reference. As you read the scenario, think about how you would have handled this situation if you were Erwin, Mary's manager.

CASE STUDY: *The Trusted Employee*

Characters

MARY	Head Bookkeeper, reports to Erwin King
ERWIN KING	Controller, reports to company president
TIM	Sales Manager
VICKI, DORIS	Clerks

The company has about 300 employees.

Action

Sales Manager Tim, dressed for travel, visits head bookkeeper Mary in her office to get a travel advance.

MARY: You know the rules, Tim. No cash advance for a trip until you turn in your expense report for the last one.

TIM: Mary, I'd love to. But my plane leaves in 45 minutes. C'mon, if Erwin hassles you about it, I'll take the heat.

MARY: Okay. But I want both reports the day you get back.

[Mary begins counting out cash into Tim's palm.]

Three hundred, three-fifty, four hundred. Sign here for the cash advance.

TIM: *[Puts the cash in his wallet and picks up his bags.]*

Gotta run. Is your mother any better?

MARY: About the same. But at least she's home now. Thanks for asking, Tim.

[Two clerks Vicki and Doris enter—the wall clock reads 8:40—as they go quickly to their desks.]

VICKI: Mr. King's not in yet, is he?

MARY: He has been for half an hour. When he says 8:30, he means at your desk and working—not just arriving at work.

DORIS: The sales people come and go whenever they feel like it.

MARY: You know they travel and work late hours.

DORIS: Show up early. . . work late. Is that how you made it from clerk to head bookkeeper?

MARY: It didn't hurt. Doris, do you have last month's expense reports and cash advance records? I can't find them.

DORIS: Mr. King took them out of the file yesterday.

ERWIN: *[from the doorway of his of office.]*

Mary, will you step in here for a moment?

MARY: Right away, Mr. King.

ERWIN: *[to Mary as she enters and closes the door]*

Please have a seat. As you know, Price Waterhouse comes in next week for its half-year audit, and . . .

MARY: . . . If you are concerned about Tim's overdue expense report, I just spoke with him this morning. He knows that Thursday is the absolute deadline.

ERWIN: Actually, I'm more concerned about other expense reports. Mary, you've worked for me enough years to know what a stickler I am for expense reporting. And, that my first rule is they have to be done in ink.

MARY: I keep after them, Mr. King, but lately . . .

ERWIN: There are four or five examples here of questionable erasures, mostly for cash advances. Ring any bells?

MARY: *[quickly]* No.

[As they stare at each other for a moment, Mary starts to sob.]

Yes . . . it rings a lot of bells. My mother's first hospital stay was a financial disaster. But this last one wiped me out. I borrowed to the limit from banks, relatives, even friends. I was still short of what I needed to check her out of Huntington Memorial and bring her home.

ERWIN: So your answer was dipping into petty cash?

PHASE I: EXPLORE (continued)

MARY: Yes.

ERWIN: How much?

MARY: Exactly seven hundred dollars. I planned to replace it, a hundred a month, until it was all back. I know you're disappointed.

ERWIN: Shocked, is more like it. You paid your dues here, studied evenings, moved up to head our bookkeeping unit. You've been the model of how our employees should perform . . . up to this point.

MARY: It won't happen again.

ERWIN: This is extremely serious. I can't ignore it. Mary, you violated the basic trust a controller has to have in a bookkeeper.

MARY: I'll earn that trust back, you'll see . . .

ERWIN: My inclination, frankly, is dismissal. But in view of your hard work and loyalty for seven years, I'll talk with Henry, the president, before making a decision. Don't discuss our conversation with anyone. I'll let you know in the morning.

MARY: [*as she leaves Erwin's office*] Yes sir.

YOUR RESPONSE

If you were the president of this organization, when Erwin consulted you, what would you say to him? What is your reasoning?

_____

_____

_____

_____

_____

STEP 1. CLARIFY CRITICAL ISSUES

We'll return both to your personal disagreement and "The Trusted Employee" case as we look at the three steps of the Explore Phase.

To start your diagnostic exploration of a budding disagreement, determine if your initial views on core issues are shared by other stakeholders.

The key is *honest feedback.* However, when the people you count on are in a hierarchical role relationship (such as boss-subordinate, teacher-student, parent-child), they may not feel safe expressing disagreement. They may not want to risk saying, "I feel you're wrong" or even, "I see this issue differently." Subordinates, for example, may not want to take a position that might hurt their careers. They don't want to have their views brushed aside, or be seen as odd or uncooperative. Subordinates generally accept as a self-evident truth the maxim, confirmed by social psychologists: You create less trouble for yourself by agreeing with your boss. Therefore, *don't expect critical feedback to be freely volunteered.* To learn views that differ from your own, you can do the following:

▶ *Model the desired level of openness,* allowing yourself to be appropriately vulnerable. For example, if warranted by the situation, express your own fears, doubts and concerns.

▶ *Ask for feedback*—and don't punish those who then tell you something you didn't want to hear.

▶ *Explain why you want feedback*—for example, to stimulate innovation, realize mutual gain, or create a more satisfying relationship.

▶ *Look for nonverbal cues,* especially from people who may not feel comfortable articulating their disagreement. Notice if verbal and nonverbal messages are *congruent.* For example, is your boss saying, "Take all the time you need," while she nervously packs her briefcase and glances at her watch?

To learn where the views of others diverge from your own, *help them to disagree with you.*

STEP 2. IDENTIFY STAKEHOLDERS

Think about your own potential conflict—the one you've described. Write the names of those persons who have a vested interest in the outcome of the events in your narrative. Include individuals who have to implement decisions or live with them. Indicate each stake holder's position or relationship to you. (Note: You usually will want to take this Step concurrently with Step 1.)

Stakeholder 's Name	*Position or Relationship*

The stakeholders in the "Trusted Employee" scenario were:

Lead Bookkeeper Mary   Controller Erwin King

President Henry   Board of Directors

Stockholders   Auditor Price Waterhouse

Other Employees

NOTE: While your list of stakeholders may be limited to your main "characters," also consider others who are likely to be most concerned with or affected by the resolution of your disagreement.

STEP 3. ASSESS SOURCES OF CONFLICT

Seeds of conflict include stakeholder perception that proposed action is based on:

> Distorted or Incomplete Information
>
> Wrong or Incompatible Goals
>
> Ineffective or Inappropriate Methods
>
> Antagonistic or Other Negative Feelings

Explore your disagreement by probing each of these categories as suggested on the following pages.

Potential Source of Conflict:
Distorted or Incomplete Information

To avoid distorted or incomplete information answer these questions:

▶ Do stakeholders have full *access to the same information?* For example, are upper-level managers missing critical operating details or the most current data? Have estimates been exaggerated to make someone look good—such as a favored vendor? Are less informed employees missing part of the big picture? (Like blind men feeling different parts of an elephant and drawing vastly different conclusions about the nature of the animal.)

▶ Is the same information being *interpreted differently?* Perceptions are influenced by social conditioning, personal history and vested interests. One person interprets an event as a challenging opportunity, another sees it as a threat. One person sees long-term savings in a proposal, another sees immediate higher costs.

STEP 3. ASSESS SOURCES OF CONFLICT (continued)

Write below, *for your situation*, how you will assure that the stakeholders have *accurate and complete information*.

_____

_____

_____

_____

_____

To assure they had accurate information in "The Trusted Employee" case, Erwin asked Mary for a copy of her hospital receipt to determine if Mary had, in fact, paid the $700 as she claimed. Erwin also examined earlier expense reports for erasures or other signs of alteration to determine if Mary's offense was a one-time aberration.

Potential Source of Conflict: Wrong or Incompatible Goals

When the goals of interdependent people diverge or clash, hopeless disagreement is *not* inevitable. Disagreement over goals usually occurs at *one level* of concern. However, a higher level can almost always be found where stakeholders share a common vision or goal. Identify the *common ground*. It's a solid starting point where agreement already exists.

For example, labor and management may disagree over wages, but if both parties agree that a primary goal is for the organization to remain viable, a foundation to build on is in place.

Write below, *for your situation*, superordinate goals that are in agreement with stakeholder needs and wants.

_____

_____

_____

_____

_____

_____

_____

_____

In "The Trusted Employee" case, Erwin's and Henry's goals may clash. Erwin believes it is the responsibility of a Certified Public Accountant to fire anyone who is dishonest. Henry questions whether dismissal is fair if compelling extenuating circumstances exist. However, at another level, Erwin and Henry do agree on two superordinate goals. They want employees who can be trusted; and they want an effective and efficient system for handling petty cash.

STEP 3. ASSESS SOURCES OF CONFLICT (continued)

Potential Source of Conflict:
Ineffective or Inappropriate Methods

Disagreement may exist over methods for completing a task—the techniques and procedures that different people prefer. The following diagnostic checklist can aid you in identifying and examining disagreement associated with methods.

☐ Does good *alignment* exist between a task to be accomplished and the people asked to perform it? That is, are the skills and interests of individuals well matched to the activities they are asked to undertake?

☐ Is the required task *well-framed?* Specifically, have clear and reasonable boundaries been set? Are the responsibilities coordinated so they mesh well? Has adequate authority been delegated?

☐ Is enough *support* being provided? Do people have adequate resources, facilities, training and recognition? Do they have appropriate input into decisions that affect their efforts?

☐ Are acceptable *ethical standards* being followed? Do employees use their organizational position for personal benefit? Are moral standards advocated but not practiced? For example, if a father preaches obey-the-law to his children, does he also buy a radar detector for his car so he won't get caught speeding?

Disagreement over methods entails three factors:

#1. How people weigh the odds that one procedure will be more effective than another in reaching a common goal.

#2. How people assess personal costs. For example, a method acceptable to one person may be so time consuming that another person can't pursue other higher-priority goals.

#3. Personal values and ethical concerns.

For your situation, write below the issues you want to examine more deeply regarding methods and values.

_____

_____

_____

_____

_____

_____

In "The Trusted Employee" case, Henry decided to explore the way Mary went about meeting her need for cash. Why didn't she ask Erwin for counsel during the two-year period her mother was seriously ill? Had Erwin been too aloof to his employees? Why weren't employees following the written instructions about completing their expense reports in ink? How could the company's method of handling cash be improved for better efficiency and less temptation? Should a written policy for making loans to employees be developed or a credit union affiliation made? Is an Employee Assistance Program needed? Is Ajax Company morally responsible for making the issues public by charging embezzlement in a court of law?

STEP 3. ASSESS SOURCES OF CONFLICT (continued)

Potential Source of Conflict: Antagonistic or Other Negative Feelings

Disagreement, when it surfaces, may have a long history. Left-over resentment from previously mismanaged conflicts tends to linger. People who have been demeaned or feel betrayed may act in punishing ways to "even" the score. When disagreement stems from old wounds, it may be difficult to diagnose because it rarely is acknowledged and often masquerades as a "personality clash."

Not all negative feelings come from interpersonal conflict. Other sources include discouragement with general inefficiency, or frustration from intergroup rivalry.

As you diagnose your *situation*, write how long the disagreement you described may have been incubating, if those involved appear to be rivals, and if other negative emotions likely lie below the surface.

_____

_____

_____

_____

In "The Trusted Employee" case, when Mary moved into positions of greater responsibility, perhaps she didn't feel adequately compensated. If her communication with her boss was poor, and the facts suggest this possibility, Mary's stealing may have been influenced by feelings of resentment and the rationale: "it's money I should have been getting all along anyway."

NOTE: In the exploration phase, you are attempting to ferret out all *potential causes* of disagreement. You may raise more questions than you need to resolve immediately. For example, to handle Mary's petty cash, it was not necessary to start a credit union or extend insurance coverage. However, the sooner diagnostic questions are addressed, the sooner you will be in a position to avert needless future conflict.

PHASE II: PLAN

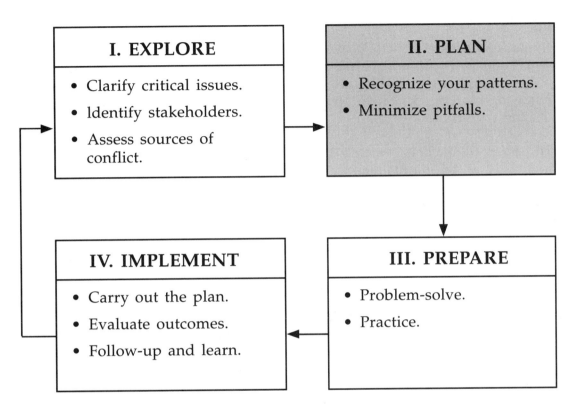

I. EXPLORE	II. PLAN
• Clarify critical issues. • Identify stakeholders. • Assess sources of conflict.	• Recognize your patterns. • Minimize pitfalls.
IV. IMPLEMENT	III. PREPARE
• Carry out the plan. • Evaluate outcomes. • Follow-up and learn.	• Problem-solve. • Practice.

Your exploration phase framed the central issues, identified stakeholders, and suggested likely sources of disagreement. At this point, you are ready to plan a strategic approach for dealing with relevant differing views.

THE FIRST STEP IS TO RECOGNIZE YOUR PATTERNS

STEP 1. RECOGNIZE YOUR PATTERNS

Most people bring relatively *stable patterns of behavior, or styles*, to the resolution of disputes. The common element in all of your disagreements is you. Therefore, start by gathering information about your own typical behavior. Although it's difficult to see yourself as others see you, the following exercises will help you recognize patterns you've developed for dealing with conflict.

To benefit fully, complete each exercise as though you are personally involved and have a real stake in the outcome.

EXERCISE: "Allocating Fixed Resources"

Assume you are one of three people who will be given $1,000 if you are willing to play a game and abide by its rules. The fourth person in the game is a timekeeper. The *rules are: You* and the two other players are to meet and each will receive $1,000. At this meeting, with no pre-liminary discussion, you have a maximum of 7 minutes to re-allocate the group's $3,000. However, one of you is to leave the meeting with no money. The other two players may divide the $3,000 in any fashion. No hidden deals are allowed—that is, you can't arrange to pay off one person if he or she drops a claim to a share of the money during the game. The timekeeper will announce the time remaining at one-minute intervals. If seven minutes elapse and the re-allocation hasn't been completed in accordance with the rules—then, the timekeeper gets the entire $3,000.

Imagine yourself as one of the three players. (Better yet, you may want to try the game with friends, using play money or smaller dollar amounts. For example, each player might contribute $20 and, for realism at least one person doesn't get it back.) Write below the approach or *strategy you plan to use.*

_____

_____

_____

_____

_____

_____

_____

_____

_____

STEP 1. RECOGNIZE YOUR PATTERNS (continued)

Two initial strategies are most common. Interestingly, the most popular one almost always fails and sooner or later is abandoned. It's a *selling* approach. That is, one player tries to convince the other two that his or her needs are the most worthy or the most desperate. When persuasion fails, as it usually does—because it's hard to convince anyone to walk away from $1,000—the players often switch to a second strategy. They agree on a *decision rule* that appears fair. The usual rule is some form of lottery, like a short straw or odd coin out. On rare occasions, *force is* used—that is, one person grabs the money and holds it for seven minutes. Finally, some players *collaborate*, asking: Can we turn this win-lose game into a win-win situation? They sometimes discover a charity to which they can all agree to make a donation. Then, they typically give everything to a player who appears trustworthy for contribution to the charity.

The intent of this exercise, and those that follow, is not to get the "right" answer—but to look for patterns.

What was your preferred strategy? Did you select a *selling* approach to convince the other players that your needs were most compelling? Did you propose a *decision rule* to stop the clock. Did you settle your differences by domination using force or threats? Did you consider a *collaborative* strategy to reach a superordinate goal?

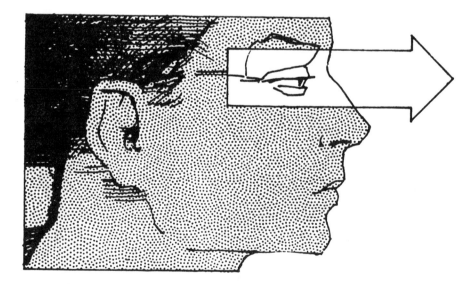

The exercise on the following page applies to an organizational setting. Again, it enables you to collect additional information about your preferred styles for managing disagreement.

EXERCISE: *"Personal Business At Work"*

This case concerns a subordinate doing personal work in the office. Assume you are this employee's boss. After reading the case, *rank* the five options—A through E in the spaces provided. Use "1" to indicate the *most* appropriate option; "5" for the *least* appropriate option.

> As supervisor of a 12-person design section, you notice that one of your designers is drafting plans for an addition to her house. She is an employee whose competence and initiative you value. When you ask why she's working on a personal project during company hours, she says that she has caught up on all high-priority work and lacks adequate drafting equipment at home. You also know she has done some nondrafting work on rush projects for the company on her own time at home.

Rank your options below.

A. ____ Tell the designer exactly what you think and feel, and invite her also to be frank. Then say you are willing to take the time to work out a mutually agreeable plan.

B. ____ In a friendly way, tell the designer that you understand her thinking. Then sell her on not working on personal projects in the office because of the precedent it sets for other employees who may not be as willing as she to do work at home.

C. ____ Ignore the situation. Deal with future problems, if any, when they come up.

D. ____ Offer to let the designer continue to use the equipment for personal projects, but only after hours, during lunchtime, or on weekends.

E. ____ Inform the designer that the company has a policy against doing personal projects during the workday.

You can extend this exercise by asking one or more friends or colleagues to provide their rankings independently of one another. Then see, as a group, if you can arrive at a single group ranking. If the deliberations drag on, set a time limit. Notice what processes you use in attempting to gain group agreement.

During group discussions, based on this option-ranking exercise, participants expressed the views indicated on the next page. Their comments illustrate the widely diverse views that capable people can generate.

STEP 1. RECOGNIZE YOUR PATTERNS (continued)

Option Pros and Cons

Option A   Tell the designer exactly what you think and feel, and invite her also to be frank. Then say you are willing to take the time to work out a mutually agreeable plan.

Comments

For: In this *collaborative* strategy, the subordinate feels respected by her boss because her views are honored as they work out a mutually agreeable plan.

Against: This is a weak management style in which the boss fails to take responsibility for what must be done.

Option B   In a friendly way, tell the designer that you understand her thinking. Then sell her on not working on personal projects in the office because of the precedent it sets for their employees who may not be as willing as she to do work at home.

Comments

For: This option enables the boss to *smooth* over differences without wasting time in long, fruitless debate.

Against: The boss doesn't get the benefit of the employee's views, and may discourage her future initiative.

Option C   Ignore the situation. Deal with future problems, if any, when they come up.

Comments

For: When 12 people work together for any period of time, everyone knows the diligent employees who take work home. There's no danger of setting a troublesome precedent. As the saying does, "If something isn't broken, don't fix it."

Against: This *maintenance* strategy, by inaction, tacitly accepts the subordinate's behavior and creates an undesirable precedent that may escalate in the future.

Option D Offer to let the designer continue to use the equipment for personal projects, but only after hours, during lunchtime, or on weekends.

Comments

For: In this *bargaining* strategy, the boss gains good will with the employee by allowing her to satisfy a personal need without violating policy and at minimal cost to the organization.

Against: The boss may unknowingly be subjecting the company to potential liability. For example, if the employee hurts herself while at work during a weekend without supervision, the company may be liable.

Option E Tell the designer there is a policy against doing personal projects during the workday.

Comments

For: Following a specific company *rule* definitively settles the issue. By enforcing all company policies, irrespective of the situation, the organization is not liable to being sued in the future for discrimination or favoritism.

Against: For the boss simply to recite a company policy, leaves the employee feeling her boss doesn't really care about her competence, loyalty or initiative. It's a turn off.

This, and the previous exercise, are designed to stimulate your thinking about how to deal with others who hold views different from your own.

Turn your attention again to your scoring of your *Management* Of *Differences Inventory* (MODI-Self).

STEP 2. MINIMIZE PITFALLS

"Red Shoes" is the story of a woman who, when she puts on red ballet shoes, dances like a magnificent prima ballerina, but is unable to stop dancing. This metaphor warns that any style we master can be both a blessing and a potential trap.

When we become proficient at anything, we tend to overuse our skill. In childhood, when something works really well, we repeat it. Throughout life, people overuse superior skills even in situations where they are inappropriate; and neglect developing fledgling skills even where they would be most useful. When, irrespective of the resultant outcome, one persists in a stable, predictable behavior, others see this preferred pattern as a *personal style*.

In contrast, the term *strategic approach* will be reserved for those behaviors that you *consciously choose* to produce a desired outcome.

EXERCISE: *Neglecting or Overusing Approaches to Resolving Conflict*

Your scores on MODI-Self reflect approaches to managing disagreement that you may overly depend upon or, conversely, you may neglect. Your effectiveness in dealing with disagreement requires that you deliberately choose appropriate approaches for each specific situation, rather than use a reactive or habitual style.

To determine if you have a pattern of over- or underusing available approaches, compare your scores on MODI-Self with the mean scores of 275 managers from industry, government, and nonprofit organizations. If any of your scores are 3 *or more points below the mean, you* probably are *underusing* these approaches. If your score is 3 *or more points above, you* may be *overusing* these approaches. (For the statistically minded reader, one standard deviation is about 3 points.)

For any scores 3 points higher (suggesting *overuse)* or lower (suggesting *neglect)* than the mean, you'll find the following questions helpful in over-coming automatic reactions, building self-awareness, and broadening your repertoire. For easy comparison, write your scores in the spaces below.

MAINTAIN

Manager Mean Score = 10.7   *Your Score* = _____

If neglected: Do you take the time to collect enough background information? Do you let emotions cool before taking action?

If overused: Do you wait so long to act that you're seen as unwilling to take reasonable risks? While you gather data, do problems tend to escalate?

SMOOTH

Manager Mean Score = 11.7   *Your Score* = _____

If neglected: Are you often unable to persuade others or have trouble selling good ideas?

If overused: Do your selling tactics appear to others as manipulative?

EXERCISE (continued)

DOMINATE

Manager Mean Score = 11.1   *Your Score =* _____

If neglected: Are you seen as a person who doesn't take a firm stand or have deep convictions? Do you command enough control when you need it?

If overused: Are you seen as pushy, or uncaring about the ideas of others? Have others become too dependent on you? Have you stifled initiative?

DECIDE BY RULE

Manager Mean Score = 12.0   *Your Score =* _____

If neglected: Do you waste time discussing differences that really aren't important and get too personally involved in their resolution?

If overused: Do you appear aloof and unwilling to take the heat of direct confrontation by relying too heavily on impersonal methods to resolve disagreements?

COEXIST

Manager Mean Score = 12.2   *Your Score =* _____

If neglected: Are you willing to tolerate ambiguity and able to keep several balls in the air? Are you willing to risk being proved wrong by the results of parallel experiments?

If overused: Do you waste time and resources by allowing too many experiments to run for too long?

BARGAIN

Manager Mean Score = 13.7   *Your Score =* _____

If neglected: Are others taking advantage of your tendency not to push hard enough to win the best deal?

If overused: Do others start discussions with you by inflating their needs because they anticipate that you will press for concessions?

YIELD

Manager Mean Score = 10.6   *Your Score =* _____

If neglected: Are you seen as uncooperative, not a team player? Are you so often unyielding that your views are discounted?

If overused: Are you seen as an "apple polisher" more concerned with ingratiating than advocating what you truly believe?

RELEASE

Manager Mean Score = 11.1   *Your Score =* _____

If neglected: Do you let others learn from their own experience? Do you help others develop their initiative?

If overused: In helping others to develop, are you taking excessive risks or abdicating your responsibilities?

COLLABORATE

Manager Mean Score = 14.5   *Your Score =* _____

If neglected: Are others demotivated by your failure to invite their participation in decisions that significantly affect them? Are you missing creative perspectives by not exploring differing views?

If overused: Do you avoid taking personal responsibility by using a "committee" approach? Do you waste too much time holding meetings?

Reflecting on these critical questions will help you challenge your reactive patterns and identify the approach, or blend of approaches, that fit the unique needs of each situation you encounter.

PHASE III: PREPARE

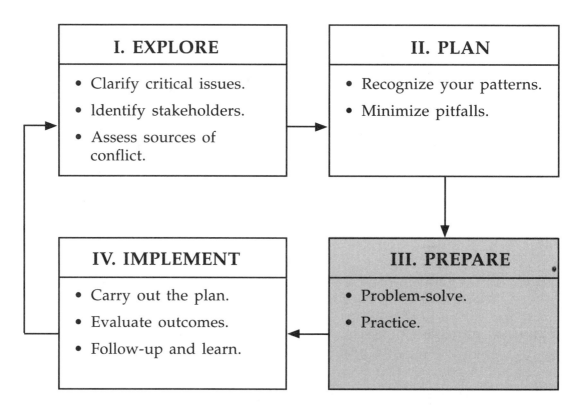

I. EXPLORE	II. PLAN
• Clarify critical issues. • Identify stakeholders. • Assess sources of conflict.	• Recognize your patterns. • Minimize pitfalls.
IV. IMPLEMENT	III. PREPARE
• Carry out the plan. • Evaluate outcomes. • Follow-up and learn.	• Problem-solve. • Practice.

Two important steps remain prior to implementation: (1) develop your strategic approach within a problem-solving framework; and (2) practice — with a little help from your friends.

CASE STUDY AHEAD . . . .

STEP 1. PROBLEM-SOLVE

Applying the Guiding Principles, Nine Strategic Approaches, and Four-Phase Process makes good sense. However, compelling logic in the heat of an argument is easy to forget. Consider the following scenario.

CASE STUDY: *Getting Started*

Characters

GEORGE   Husband

MARTHA   Wife

Action

George and Martha, after five years of marriage, are having an after-dinner "discussion" in the sparsely furnished living room of their apartment. They are standing.

GEORGE: *[in an angry voice]*

I don't believe my ears! You waited until now, the last possible minute, to tell me you're enrolling in college for the coming semester? Don't you think you should have at least talked it over with me first? How come suddenly you have to be Ms. Martha Coed?

MARTHA: Don't get so worked up. We still have a day or two before I have to send in the enrollment forms.

GEORGE: I don't get it. You haven't been inside a classroom in five years. Why, suddenly, is it such a top priority for you to get your degree? I'm struggling to get my business off the ground, and you know we need your salary.

MARTHA: Look George, I know how hard you are working, and you know how much I've wanted to go back to school. I haven't enrolled yet. I just did some checking and learned that my old academic credits are still good— but only if I go back to school during the next two years.

GEORGE: O.K., O.K. I got it. So why start now? Hold off for two years and we'll be able to afford it.

STEP 1. PROBLEM-SOLVE (continued)

MARTHA: The truth is I'm totally bored at work and I can't go on like this. I'm not going to keep my career on hold. I need to make some changes. Ever since you quit your job to become an entrepreneur, you've become a workaholic stick-in-the-mud. There's no fun left in our marriage.

GEORGE: Is that a threat?

MARTHA: I'm simply telling you how I feel. Take it any way you like. For the first time in years, I feel some excitement. Just the idea of getting some intellectual stimulation in my life is a turn-on.

GEORGE: Can we get logical here? The point I'm trying to make is the longer you wait to go back to school, the easier it will be for me to pay your tuition and for us to have some fun times again. Doesn't that make sense?

MARTHA: Yeah, it makes logical sense, but my feelings say "no." I want to grow, be challenged and stretch. I don't want to stick with a boring job while my life ticks away.

GEORGE: The bottom line, sweetie, is we can't afford to have you go back to school now. I'm working twelve hours a day for our future. I need to buy new equipment just to stay in business.

MARTHA: When we agreed you would start the business, you never mentioned my not being able to go back to school! You know I've been counting on it. Now you're backing out. I've been at the same dull job since we got married.

GEORGE: If you can just hang on for one more year . . .

MARTHA: How do I know anything will be better then? I want a life!

YOUR VIEWS

1. As George, what would be your approach to reaching a constructive resolution? As Martha, what approach would be most constructive? What do you see as the main issues that Martha and George need to resolve?

_____

_____

_____

_____

_____

_____

_____

STEP 1. PROBLEM-SOLVE (continued)

2. Continue to write dialogue (start with George's response to Martha's last statement and continue until you reach some resolution).

GEORGE: _____

_____

_____

_____

MARTHA: _____

_____

_____

_____

GEORGE: _____

_____

_____

_____

MARTHA: _____

_____

_____

_____

CASE ANALYSIS

Let's review the "Getting Started" scenario by analyzing the dialogue using the *Guiding Principles* and *Systematic Process* for managing disagreement. (You may recognize the names "Martha" and "George" were borrowed from the play *Who's Afraid Of Virginia Woolf* to accentuate the couple's discord.)

Guiding Principles for Managing Disagreement

PRESERVE DIGNITY AND RESPECT

This principle is violated by George when he refers to his wife as Ms. Coed. His "Can we get logical?" is another dig at Martha.

LISTEN WITH EMPATHY

As George listens to Martha, instead of first putting himself in her shoes and hearing her feelings, he becomes defensive, saying: "Is that a threat?" Additionally, George may not have listened carefully or caringly to Martha who reminds him: "You *know* how much I've wanted to go back to school."

FIND COMMON GROUND

The common ground, which isn't reflected in the conversation, is a loving relationship. Against the backdrop of that common intention, Martha and George would be on the same "team" rather than adversaries.

HONOR DIVERSITY

By taking their different views as opportunities for exploring creative possibilities, George may find new ways to operate the business, and Martha may find new avenues for putting more zest in her life.

STEP 1. PROBLEM-SOLVE (continued)

Process for Managing Disagreement

The initial steps of the four-phase process constitute a problem-solving framework for managing disagreements. You can apply these steps to the "Getting Started" case using reasoning similar to the following analysis.

✓ CLARIFY CRITICAL ISSUES

What's awry between Martha and George is the gap between what is and what's wanted. What's explicitly wanted and missing is *adequate financing for the business* if Martha leaves her job, preparing for a more *interesting career*. What's *implicitly* wanted, and seems from the dialogue to be missing, is respectful communication that can support a *satisfying marital relationship*.

✓ IDENTIFY STAKEHOLDERS

In this case, the stakeholders are obviously the two marital partners. Sometimes, in addition to the protagonists, others need to be considered—such as, in this case, marital, career and small business counselors.

✓ ASSESS LIKELY SOURCES OF CONFLICT

► The business needs more capital than it can generate

Possibilities: Apply for a loan. Seek outside funding. Reduce cash needs by leasing rather than buying new equipment. Reduce expenses by replacing an employee with Martha who, with her agreement, would work at least part-time in the business.

► Martha wants a more exciting job and she wants to develop more of her career potential.

Possibilities: Make George's business *the family's* business with Martha a full partner. Martha could take courses that would help her contribute to the success of the business. She could also apply for a college student loan.

✓ RECOGNIZE PATTERNS AND MINIMIZE BLOCKS

Their dialogue suggests that Martha and George have a competitive pattern going. Instead of exploring and supporting each other's needs, both husband and wife use dysfunctional personal styles. Martha with-holds information until it's so late that George appears to be selfish. George plays "Big Daddy," saying: "I'm struggling to get my business off the ground... so that I can enroll you in the best college around." Both collude in this father-daughter role pattern, which feeds their competitive power struggle.

✓ PLAN YOUR STRATEGIC APPROACH

The polarized positions (George's business versus Martha's schooling) taken by the couple leave room only for a competitive strategy, such as *bargaining*. Bargaining is appropriate for a labor-management dispute, but it doesn't foster closeness in an intimate relationship. In contrast, *collaboration* enables the partners to directly confront the disagreement by fully disclosing their needs and concerns. Through collaboration, George and Martha can diagnose the real problems, deal with blocks, and resolve the issues creatively and with good-will.

As you reread the dialogue you wrote for George and Martha, did you use a problem-solving framework? Most people don't. Constructive conflict resolution takes practice, especially in emotional situations.

STEP 2. PRACTICE

The following exercise helps you practice a full *range* of strategies and build confidence by *role playing* approaches you currently underuse.

Here's where you can use help from your friends because *two other people* are needed. If you are not in a training workshop, enlist two friends or colleagues, and teach them each of the nine strategies for managing disagreement.

Start each role play by announcing the strategic approach you intend to practice. While you will use blends in real situations, at this point, practice with a *single approach* in each role play to gain mastery.

To prepare for your role play, you may recall an event that actually happened or rehearse a disagreement that you anticipate. Alternatively, you may prefer to use the situations presented in subsequent pages. Note that each role play situation is purposely sketchy so you can add information pertinent to actual circumstances in your work and personal life. Before starting your role play, review it with your colleagues to be sure they understand your situation and objectives.

Ask one person to play the "other party" or "foil" who will provide the differing point of view. The "foil" should not too-quickly abandon his or her position, but should keep the dispute going for as long as would be realistic under the circumstances. On the other hand, when the "skill-builder" moves fully into the desired strategic approach, the foil should respond constructively.

Ask your other friend to take the role of the "observer." The observer is to witness without comment and is encouraged to take brief notes based on the *Observer Guide*, which follows the practice situations.

The *Observer Guide is* a valuable resource, worth careful review. It describes *observable behaviors* associated with each of the nine strategic approaches when they are skillfully used.

If your friends want a turn, simply rotate roles until each person has held all three positions: the skill-builder, the foil, and the observer. Following each role play, allow a few minutes for note-taking and feedback. Notice if the skill-builder slipped out of the approach he or she intended to practice and into a familiar style.

EXERCISE: Strategic Approach Trials

Approach 1: Maintain

► You just received upsetting news from home that deserves your immediate personal attention. A moment later, your secretary tells you a major client has arrived for an appointment you set up, to discuss a controversial issue on which only you have authority to resolve. Something must be said to this client.

► A new customer phones your secretary and threatens to sue your organization for an injury that occurred while the customer was allegedly using a product your company manufactures. You made the sale. Your secretary rings the call through to your office, and you pick up the phone.

Approach 2: Smooth

► Recently, you started receiving personal phone calls during working hours. While you've enjoyed these calls, you realize they are interfering with your work. You decided they may hurt your career if they continue. When you receive your next personal call, you say: ". . .

► A customer phones and insists that you personally handle the specific details of a transaction, as you have in the past. However, since your last contact with this excellent customer—you have been promoted. Your secretary tried to explain that your new position has taken you out of the customer-relations area, but without success. Now it's up to you to speak with this customer.

STEP 2. PRACTICE (continued)

Approach 3: Dominate

▶ Your car was repaired and you were assured by the garage mechanic that the problem was remedied. When you took a test drive around the block, it seemed okay, and you paid your bill. Three days later, the old symptoms recurred, indicating to you that the problem was not correctly diagnosed. You return to the garage, want your car repaired promptly and properly, and you don't intend to make an additional payment.

▶ Your company president was appointed to the executive board of United Way, a community charity. She is eager to have all employees contribute. Probably because of the president's full-employee-participation target, the company Fund Committee has been zealous to the point of becoming obnoxious. The Committee sent you three memos despite your polite but firm "not this year" replies. The Fund Committee chairman just walked into your office unannounced to convince you personally to make a donation. You intend to tell him to stop badgering you.

Approach 4: Decide By Rule

▶ You plan on buying a car soon. To date, you've collected information on prices, safety, gasoline consumption, features, reliability, road handling, resale value, maintenance costs and styling. Your family is getting impatient with your data-gathering activities, and everyone wants to have some input into the final decision. You would be happy with any one of three cars. (Role play with one "family member.")

▶ At work, a rush project has come up that needs two people to work overtime this coming weekend. Of those reporting to you, five want to work on the project to earn the extra pay. All five are equally capable of handling the job. The work can't be divided. (Role play with one "representative" employee.)

Approach 5: Coexist

► Mothers-in-law are often portrayed as difficult, overbearing people. Your relationship with your mother-in-law fits this stereotypical image perfectly. If you say "black," she says "white." She is visiting for the weekend and has just lectured you on how to bring up your children. Despite your discomfort with her views, she spared no detail on what you are doing wrong and the dire consequences to your children's future development. You respond to her monologue by saying: ". . .

► Your department is using a system for inventory control that worked well for many years. Your recently completed analysis, however, convinces you that the system should be updated. You predict added flexibility and substantial savings. Carmen is also a department manager, and her unit operates in parallel with your group. She disagrees with your analysis. Her concerns are employee resistance and a system that is more vulnerable to error requiring frequent repair. You've arranged to meet Carmen to discuss your differences. You start the conversation.

Approach 6: Bargain

► You've just moved to a new city to accept a position that is important to your career. Unfortunately, your car broke down beyond repair. Your job, which starts in two days, requires an automobile. A newspaper ad offers a used car well suited to your needs and tight budget. A phone call and taxi ride takes you to the car you want, but the asking price is more than you can afford. You haven't yet established credit in this city, and have only a modest down-payment with you. You decide to negotiate the purchase of this car.

(In "bargaining" scenarios, the person acting as the foil can add realism by privately developing specific bargaining goals. In this case, for example, a minimum selling price and terms of sale should be set—and told only to the observer—before the action starts.)

STEP 2. PRACTICE (continued)

▶ You've been assigned to an overseas operation with an exciting mission and top management visibility. You share a new office with a key peer, Pietro, who you discover is a smoker. You strongly object to smoke in your working space, and your company has no policy in its overseas facilities that covers this problem. You decide to speak with your new officemate.

Approach 7: Yield

▶ You agreed to support the position a colleague told you she was presenting at an important strategy meeting. During the meeting, after your friend made her presentation, a key executive forcefully criticized her plan. Instead of rallying to her defense as you had promised, you remained silent. Now, later in the day, your colleague enters your office and tells you how terribly disappointed she is with your lack of support at the meeting. You reply, saying: ". . .

▶ Your boss has been full of new ideas lately. Sadly, from your perspective, he intended to implement two that were not only off-target, but would have delayed your current project, added expense and reduced quality. On both occasions you explained to your boss why his ideas would hamper progress. Now he's come up with a third idea that you again feel is not helpful. However, not much is at stake, and the down-side consequences are minor. When asked for your views, you say: ". . .

Approach 8: Release

▶ Your daughter, Suzanne, received her college degree three months ago, landed a well-paying job, and is starting to build her savings by living rent-free at home. She feels the time has come to leave the nest and get her own apartment. When you talk with Suzanne, you plan to urge her to live at home longer to accrue more savings. You say: ". . .

▶ Barbara will take over your department when your promotion to a different operation takes effect next week. She's done an outstanding job, and you've been grooming her to assume added responsibilities. Today, she asked to meet with you to propose a departmental reorganization. While you want her to take more initiative, you disagree with Barbara's proposal, and feel it won't provide the benefits she anticipates. On the other hand, even if it isn't an improvement, the plan can't do much harm. You say to Barbara: ". . .

Approach 9: Collaborate

▶ You recently got married and, after three blissful months, are facing some cold realities. The problems in your otherwise happy relationship cluster around "practicality." You partner has overdrawn your joint bank account twice in the past month. You decide to discuss your bank account situation in particular, and household budgeting in general.

▶ Your boss, Tom, calls you into his office to discuss a project report you've been asked to submit to the executive board. Tom tells you it's okay to exaggerate progress during the last quarter. He says that this "white lie" will avoid needless embarrassing questions. Tom assures you that although the project has lagged behind schedule, those delays soon will be made up. You are uncomfortable with the ethical implication of your boss's request.

NOTE: The copyright holder grants readers permission to duplicate copies of the following Observer Guide pages for personal use.

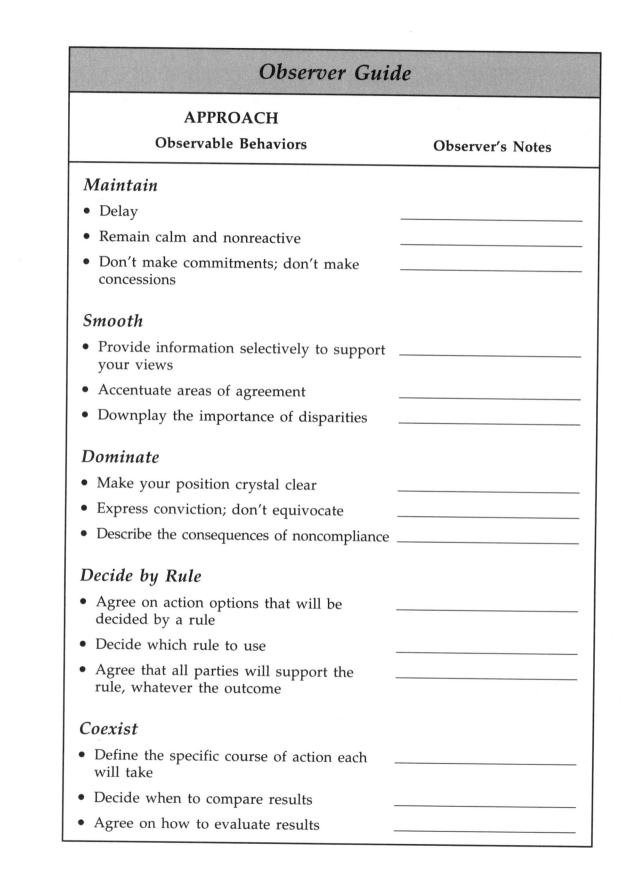

Observer Guide

APPROACH

Observable Behaviors | Observer's Notes

Maintain

- Delay
- Remain calm and nonreactive
- Don't make commitments; don't make concessions

Smooth

- Provide information selectively to support your views
- Accentuate areas of agreement
- Downplay the importance of disparities

Dominate

- Make your position crystal clear
- Express conviction; don't equivocate
- Describe the consequences of noncompliance

Decide by Rule

- Agree on action options that will be decided by a rule
- Decide which rule to use
- Agree that all parties will support the rule, whatever the outcome

Coexist

- Define the specific course of action each will take
- Decide when to compare results
- Agree on how to evaluate results

Bargain

- Clarify interests of both parties _____
- Explore "zone of mutual gain" (where _____ both parties benefit)
- Discuss compromise options _____
- Make offers and counteroffers _____

Yield

- Clarify what position you are giving up _____ and what you agree to follow
- Say what you will do or not do _____

Release

- Stipulate any reservations or limits (e.g., _____ you empower an employee, but within a given budget)
- Discuss when and how results will be _____ evaluated

Collaborate

- Disclose your interests and concerns, and _____ invite the same from the other(s)
- Listen without defending your views _____
- Problem solve without quickly converging; _____ check which action best satisfies all interests

General Notes for Observer

1. Look for congruence between verbal statements and nonverbal signals.

2. Has the disagreement been resolved?

3. If yes, is the resolution likely to be honored?

4. If no, how might the observed approach been used more effectively?

PHASE IV: IMPLEMENT

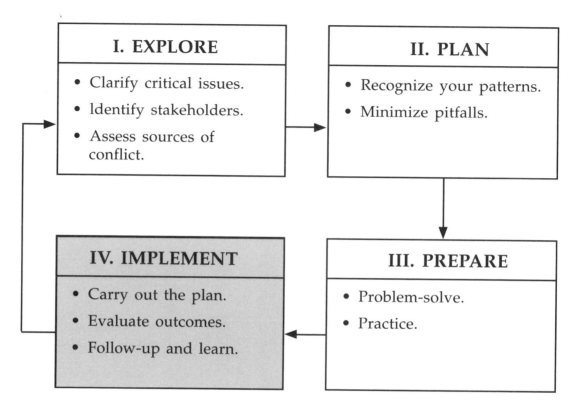

I. EXPLORE

- Clarify critical issues.
- Identify stakeholders.
- Assess sources of conflict.

II. PLAN

- Recognize your patterns.
- Minimize pitfalls.

IV. IMPLEMENT

- Carry out the plan.
- Evaluate outcomes.
- Follow-up and learn.

III. PREPARE

- Problem-solve.
- Practice.

STEP 1. CARRY OUT THE PLAN

These four considerations deserve attention in implementing your plan:

- create a productive emotional atmosphere.
- find compatible strategies and breaking deadlocks.
- build implementive skills.
- blend strategic styles and closing constructively.

The Emotional Side of Disagreement

When people disagree and voice their views, an informed decision can be made. However, many people are reluctant to express disagreement openly when they are concerned about hurting feelings or dealing with out-of-control emotional reactions.

The challenge in handling feelings is to allow them to be talked about openly. A line needs to be drawn between table-thumping rage and saying you are angry. Strong feelings can be used to bully, while unexpressed and unresolved feelings can bias good judgment. For example, some people reject good ideas when angry with the individuals expressing them.

To the extent that you disclose your feelings as you deal with differences, others will feel safer expressing what they are experiencing. You can communicate your feelings directly, saying: "I feel frustrated," "I feel embarrassed"; or by using similes, such as "I feel stepped on," "I don't feel heard."

The expression of feelings while managing disagreement serves to:

▶ *provide problem-solving feedback.* Negative feelings signal that something valued is awry.

▶ *make relevant input discussible.* When a potentially emotional topic is side-stepped, information is lost that could lead to creative solutions.

▶ *connect people more personally.* When we get to know one another as people with feelings, rather than merely as proponents of views, chances for working together constructively are improved. When we communicate our "humanness," we take a giant step toward reaching common ground.

In summary, our feelings enable others to clarify misperceptions and to join us in real, rather than role, relationships.

Managing Disagreement Constructively

STEP 1. CARRY OUT THE PLAN (continued)

Strategies That Lead to Deadlocks

If stakeholders choose strategies that don't fit together compatibly, disagreement ends in a deadlock or fragile truce. Deadlocks occur when two parties remain unyielding in their positions or keep sparring for control. For example—

▶ **Domination** is functional only when one person has the *power and resources* to direct another, the *understanding* to appreciate the situation and its implications, and a *willing follower.* In the absence of any of these conditions, dominance usually leads to the use of counter-dominance. When power is about equal, a stalemate results. When power isn't equal and the disagreement is pushed underground, it ultimately surfaces as resistance or erupts into full-blown conflict.

▶ **Smoothing** is an effective strategy when one party to the disagreement is *receptive.* On the other hand, two "smoothers" will slide into an impasse because both are selling and no one is buying. Either the arguments aren't persuasive, aren't relevant, or the people simply aren't listening to one another. A sale can't be made to those who are preoccupied with fine-tuning their own sales pitch.

Incompatibility also occurs when collaboration is opposed by *any* of the three "firm" strategies (dominate, smooth and maintain). Because collaborators are open to considering alternative views and those taking a firm position are not, the collaborator feels pushed into a corner.

USE ONE OF THE FOLLOWING APPROACHES TO BREAK THE DEADLOCK . . .

Breaking Deadlocks

To break a deadlock caused by a strategic mismatch, use one of the three "moderately flexible" approaches (bargain, coexist or decide-by-rule).

▶ **Bargaining** allows people locked in domination and counter-domination to back off. Note that while "tough battlers" resist being seen as "soft," they still can be assertive within a bargaining framework.

▶ **Coexistence** breaks an impasse when two clear options are available. In such cases, one party can pursue one course of action, while the other takes a different approach *on an experimental basis.* In advance of such an experiment, stakeholders must agree on criteria for assessing the outcomes, and when to end the experiment.

▶ **Decision-rule,** the quickest way to break a deadlock, requires identifying workable options and agreeing to a *fair and clear rule* for selecting one. For example, when kids fight over who gets which slice of pie, the dispute can be settled using as the *clear-and-fair rule:* one child cuts the pie; the other gets first pick. In the organizational world, the procedure may be a lottery, vote, seniority system, arbitration or any objective criterion.

BUILDING IMPLEMENTIVE SKILLS

Of the nine strategic approaches for managing disagreement, *two* require special attention. To *collaborate* or *bargain* successfully, *you* need interpersonal skills congruent with the character of each process. The following guidelines will help you to apply these approaches skillfully.

► **Collaboration,** also called consensual decision-making. This is a win-win strategy based on self-disclosure and mutual *trust*. All cards must be put, face up, on the table. Participant differences are resolved when they reach an agreement that reasonably satisfies all expressed needs and hopes. The following steps lead to constructive collaboration.

1. *Don't impose a solution.* The basic ground rule is that a collective view must emerge—neither from coercion nor majority vote—but from forthright, empathetic discussion.

2. *Provide background information.* Stakeholders present their views with enough background for others to understand them in context. Say what really matters to you, including your assumptions, and concerns.

3. *Don't surrender your view to reduce group tension.* If you throw in the towel to be a "nice guy" or to avoid the heat of confrontation, you deny others the benefit of your insights and reasoning.

4. *Actively invite different views.* This is not a win-lose competition. Everyone can win, but only when the richness of diverse views are honestly expressed and then creatively blended.

5. *Search deeply for understanding.* Listen to others to appreciate their insights. Honor their disclosures as you would a valued gift. Take time between responses for reflection.

6. *Keep testing ideas for group acceptance.* As you integrate ideas, keep checking to determine when relevant interests are satisfied and concerns adequately addressed.

▶ **Bargaining** is a *mixed-motive* strategy. You walk a tightrope between cooperation and competition, seeking a compromise agreement to reconcile differences. For example, two lawyers trying to settle a dispute out-of-court cooperate to save both their clients court expense. However, to win the best deal, they need to compete. Therefore, bargaining requires not the full disclosure of collaboration, but *guarded maneuvering* between "cooperative antagonists." Benjamin Franklin captured the essence of bargaining:

> "Trades would not take place unless it were advantageous to the parties concerned. Of course, it is better to strike as good a bargain as one's bargaining position permits. The worst outcome is when, by overreaching greed, no bargain is struck, and a trade that would have been advantageous to both parties does not come off at all."

Generally, you will want to deal with people who are sincere, use their power with grace, and can be counted on to honor agreements. The following guidelines offer specific suggestions for bargaining constructively.

1. *Have precise objectives and support for them.* When you know what you want and have a thoughtful rationale, your position gains *legitimacy*. If you're selling a home, for example, support your asking price with recent sales data on comparable houses in the neighborhood.

2. *Check that a mutually beneficial agreement is possible.* Probe early to discover if a *zone of mutual benefit* exists without giving away your specific goals. For buyer-seller situations, this zone would be the *price range where both would benefit*. But, within this zone, buyers jockey for a low-end price, while sellers maneuver to close the deal toward the upper end.

BUILDING IMPLEMENTIVE SKILLS
(continued)

3. *Consider a third-party mediator.* If parties are reluctant to share information directly, they may be willing to use an impartial intermediary. A third party can often assure disputants that a zone-of-mutual-benefit actually exists. Mediators also can help by: letting highly charged emotions vent; recasting issues in more acceptable terms; facilitating communication; and developing ground rules—such as holding the meeting at a neutral site and setting time limits.

4. *To strike a favorable bargain, consider the following tactics.*

   - *Give concessions grudgingly.* After you present objective standards to support your position, make only small concessions and do it reluctantly. Generous, quickly made concessions undermine your credibility.

   - *Give concessions in exchange for concessions.* Offer your concessions as "I will ____ if you will ____" When you ask for reciprocity, your nonverbal statement is, "I want to help us keep moving toward agreement, but I don't intend to give away the store in the process."

   - *Separate the issues.* You may soften resistance on critical issues if you offer concessions on issues that have only minor consequence for you. This tactic may also help the other person save face by not appearing to cave in to all your demands.

   - *Relate your bargaining stance to the other person's needs.* Instead of saying, "I need a higher salary," keep your organization's needs in mind. Say, for example, "Let me show you what I've done and will continue to do to improve the bottom line."

   - *Limit your authority.* Paradoxically, in bargaining, less authority is more power. Salespeople who can't grant discounts and buyers who can't exceed budgets don't make concessions in those areas. Also, if you have to defer to a higher authority, you gain time to think through a difficult concern.

BLENDING STRATEGIC APPROACHES

For clarity, each approach has been described as though it is implemented in its pure form. In reality, strategic approaches are often combined to create a hybrid or blend. The two most common blends are elaborated below.

Blend #1: Domination-Smoothing

This blend is effective when you want to be forceful in your conviction and persuasive in your presentation. An appropriate application is the supervision of an employee who violates a company policy. The supervisor wants to be certain the policy is followed, and also wants the employee to be convinced the policy is sound so she won't violate it covertly.

Blend #2: Bargaining-Collaboration

This is such a common blend it has its own name—*negotiation*.* Situations appropriate for this blend occur when you can help yourself by also helping the other party. If, when you start *slicing* what appears to be a fixed "pie" though bargaining, you see an opportunity for *enlarging* the pie through collaborating. This can be done by exploring common interests. For example, suppose you are bargaining over how to divide a crate of oranges. Within this bargaining framework, you can invite collaboration by disclosing: "I'm interested in oranges because I want the rind for baking. Why are you interested in them?" If the other person's answer is "Juice!" you've uncovered a juicy win-win solution.

---

*For an excellent book on negotiating, see *Successful Negotiation* by Robert Maddux, Crisp Publications.

CLOSING CONSTRUCTIVELY

Just as salespeople focus attention on closing a sale, you need to concern yourself with the final steps in translating your differences into agreement. Here are some helpful guidelines.

1. DOCUMENT YOUR ARGUMENT.

Even personal agreements between parents and children are more effective when written. A carefully typed statement demonstrates commitment and provides a reference for the future when memories get hazy.

2. DRAFT YOUR AGREEMENT AS DISCUSSIONS PROGRESS.

As you search for how to phrase your agreement, the intentions of both parties will be clarified. Participants also will see what issues, terms and conditions remain on the agenda to be resolved.

3. DECIDE HOW RESULTS WILL BE MONITORED.

What will be measured? How? By whom? For how long? What will constitute a successful outcome? Get commitments from individuals for deadlines to complete specific responsibilities.

4. DISCUSS WHAT HAPPENS IF . . .

A big "if" to consider is the possibility of nonperformance. Whether a legally binding contract or a note taped on the refrigerator door to distribute household chores, the *consequences* of not living up to the agreement should be agreed upon in advance.

5. HELP THE OTHER PERSON SELL THE AGREEMENT "BACK HOME."

Determine if your disputant needs further approval or ratification. If so, strengthen his or her hand by rehearsing arguments helpful in persuading others to go along.

6. SET A REALISTIC DEADLINE.

Is timely closure important to you? If so, indicate why. Perhaps if you don't resolve your differences by next Tuesday, you can't guarantee delivery, hold the interest rate, or assure approval. Deadlines stir action.

STEP 2. EVALUATE OUTCOMES

The purpose of evaluation is twofold:

#1. to serve as the basis for initiating *corrective or adaptive action*

#2. *to learn so* that future disagreements will be handled better

To evaluate the outcome of a disagreement, weigh results against the five criteria presented below. To demonstrate applying these criteria to a specific disagreement, let's return to *The Trusted Employee* case (see page 28).

Technical. Is the resolution you've come up with technically sound?

Example: In *The Trusted Employee* case, replacing cash advances to travelers with plastic cards for automated-teller machines is workable and convenient because the machines have 24-hour access.

Economic. Is the solution more cost-effective than the old system?

Example: The use of credit cards, versus cash advances, will save money because accounting and an audit trail are handled by the bank.

Social-Psychological. Will resolution of differences help morale?

Example: If Mary is retained, how would this flagrant abuse of one's job responsibility be viewed by other employees?

Ethical-Legal. Is the solution legal, moral and fair?

Example: The legal issue is clear: Mary embezzled company funds. Fairness may be an issue if: (1) Mary was under severe emotional duress, and (2) other employees were "stealing" from the company in different forms: long breaks, late lunches, and marginal performance.

Political. Will the resolution be supported by those in positions of power?

Example: Should executive board members be informed, to assure their support if the case becomes public.

PERSONAL LEARNING

Reflecting about how you have managed each disagreement helps build skill and self-confidence. You can guide this self-examination by reviewing each of the four phases of managing disagreements.

Phase I: Explore

Did you collect enough information? Were you impatient? Were your sources reliable?

Did you accurately pinpoint the information, goals, methods, and feelings that were at the heart of the disagreement?

Phase II: Plan

Did you consider a full range of strategic approaches and choose an appropriate one or an appropriate blend? If not, did you opt for a familiar strategy with which you are more comfortable?

Phase III: Prepare

Did you anticipate the key issues? If not, were you underprepared?

Did you respond creatively to the unexpected?

Phase IV: Implement

Were you able, in your intervention, to build an appropriate level of mutual trust and respect? If not, what got in the way?

Did you marshall adequate resources and enlist the support you needed? If not, did you operate too independently?

What did you learn?

STEP 3. FOLLOW-UP AND LEARN

Your evaluation will suggest if any follow-up activity is needed. Clearly, if the outcome is off-target, remedial action is appropriate. Even if a dispute is reconciled constructively, some monitoring and reinforcement helps assure that commitments will be diligently kept.

To catch disagreement before it escalates into conflict, you may want to design formal systems for airing grievances. In families, this can be as simple as a weekly roundtable where parents and children can discuss anything that feels off. Organizational justice systems include supervisory training in managing disagreement, a grievance appeals process, and use of an ombudsman. Empowered to speak with everyone, including top executives, the ombudsman cannot mandate action but helps clear up misunderstanding.

For your personal growth, take time to record the key points in your management of important disagreements. From these notes you will more clearly see where future improvements can be made. Identify the skills you want to develop further and follow up on them.

Section III features a case designed to help you review the key points about managing disagreement.

REVIEW CASE: IT'S YOUR TURN

SECTION

III

Summary

REVIEW CASE: SERVING THE CUSTOMER

Background

Most organizations want to realize a level of quality that satisfies or exceeds customer expectations. This aim is made more difficult because competitive pressures demand improving quality without sacrificing timely delivery or incurring extra cost. When employee apathy compounds the mission of satisfying customers, the ability to manage differences is challenged.

As you review this brief case, reflect on what you might have done if you were the marketing executive who first learned about widespread customer discontent.

Pat was recently promoted to marketing manager for Transitex, an electronics manufacturing company employing 350 workers. An ambitious young MBA graduate, Pat was eager to climb the company's career ladder.

Shortly after being promoted, Pat received calls from several irate customers. After initiating prompt corrective action, Pat decided to conduct a phone survey to learn the extent of the problem. The random sampling of recent customers indicated widespread dissatisfaction. The most common complaints: either orders were shipped late or errors were made in what was shipped. Some unhappy customers had already given their business to competitors.

Pat decided this situation had to be addressed promptly to prevent future recurrence. With support from top management, Pat created the new position of "customer coordinator" in the marketing department. This person would be responsible for systematically determining if procedures needed to be changed and initiating whatever corrective action was warranted.

When Pat distributed a company-wide memo announcing the new customer coordinator, the attitude of many long-time employees was: "This too shall pass." The company had created other improvement programs that had proven ineffectual, withered away and were later dropped.

Disappointed and frustrated by the lack of caring about what appeared to be a crisis, Pat decided to plan an aggressive strategy.

REVIEW CASE: SERVING THE CUSTOMER (continued)

YOUR RESPONSE

If you were marketing manager, how would you deal with this situation? Write your overall strategy, how you would handle conflicts, and your specific implementation plan.

_____

_____

_____

_____

_____

_____

_____

The most common responses to the situation are: shape up the shipping department; ask workers for their ideas on why shipments are going out late or are inaccurate; and, provide incentives for workers to improve their performance. While these are reasonable suggestions, the Four-Phase problem-solving framework enables your diagnosis to be richer and your plan more focused.

Process for Managing Disagreement

Phase I: Explore

► *Clarify Critical Issues*

Customers are dissatisfied, business is being lost, and employees are disgruntled.

► *Identify Stakeholders*

In addition to marketing and shipping personnel, others who may be involved in the problem include managers and staff in manufacturing, quality assurance, inventory control, and training. Executive management, financial supporters, major customers and suppliers also have a stake in the issues.

► *Assess Likely Sources of Conflict*

When a problem develops in a sequential process, it's often useful to follow the flow. In this case, the process starts when a sale is made.

Sales-related concerns that deserve exploration include:

- Have sales personnel quoted realistic delivery dates?

- Is there an adequate system for special handling of high-priority orders?

- Can sales demand be predicted more accurately so that adequate inventory levels will not create shipping delays?

Inventory-related concerns that may be part of the problem:

- Is Transitex's inventory-control system adequate?

- Are purchased components being delivered on schedule?

- Are quality assurance standards—internally and for suppliers— adequate?

REVIEW CASE: SERVING THE CUSTOMER (continued)

Shipping concerns include:

- Are shipping personnel being selected, trained and motivated appropriately?

- Are proper shippers (truckers, rail, UPS, postal service) being used?

► *Exploration of these general questions is also helpful:*

- What follow-up should be provided, to assure customer satisfaction?

- What organization, production or shipping changes, if any, were recently made that may be related to the current problems?

- What, if anything, is the competition doing differently?

Phase II: Plan

► *Recognize Patterns and Minimize Blocks*

Management seems to be following a pattern, particularly with regard to previous "improvement" programs (and violating the principle "Listen with Empathy"). Managers should check how receptively they listen, and how flexibly they respond to thoughtful alternative views.

Managers were so aloof and authoritarian in the past that workers now are apathetic and resentful. More personal involvement coupled with open-minded flexibility is needed. The resultant *collaborative* strategic approach is likely to produce constructive results. (**NOTE:** When you plan to use any strategic approach, introduce it in a manner *congruent* with the approach. For example, introduce collaboration through discussion, not by a memo directing: "This group *shall* collaborate!")

Phase III: Prepare

► *Problem-Solve*

Generate alternatives responsive to the potential causes or likely conflict sources. Examples:

- Develop a mission and values statement reflecting the company's commitment to quality, service, profitability, equitable reward systems and meaningful involvement of employees.

- Develop an integrated customer-driven program to improve sales forecasts, scheduling, inventory control, quality assurance including supplier performance, and order-fulfillment procedures.

- Initiate better department-customer-supplier coordination.

- Provide needed training.

- Design an early warning system to monitor customer satisfaction.

- Study competitor's products and services.

► *Pave the Way*

Design action with ideas from managers and staff closest to the work with input from major customers and suppliers.

As the action is being developed, those stakeholders not directly involved should be briefed. Executives should explicitly state that this program is top priority because the company's ability to remain competitive is at risk.

Phase IV: Implement

► *Carry Out The Plan, Evaluate Outcomes, Learn*

Implement the plan, monitor results from the perspectives of all stakeholders. If agreements are working, capture the learning. If something is off, use the five evaluation criteria to pinpoint dysfunctions—technical, economic, social-psychological, legal-ethical, and political—and make midcourse corrections.

SUMMARY REVIEW

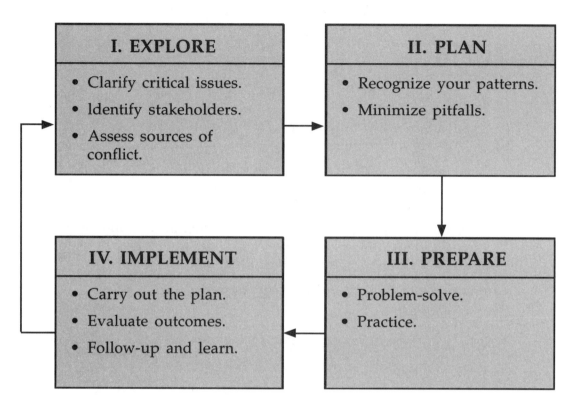

I. EXPLORE	II. PLAN
• Clarify critical issues. • Identify stakeholders. • Assess sources of conflict.	• Recognize your patterns. • Minimize pitfalls.

IV. IMPLEMENT	III. PREPARE
• Carry out the plan. • Evaluate outcomes. • Follow-up and learn.	• Problem-solve. • Practice.

I. EXPLORE

► **Clarify Critical Issues**   After you've developed your initial position, determine if others agree with your views. If not, identify areas of difference on key issues.

► **Identify Stakeholders**   Who are those with a vested interest in the outcome of the disagreement?

► **Assess Likely Sources of Conflict**   Check roles, goals, boundaries, old wounds, mistrust, misunderstanding, power struggles, unmet expectations and assumptions.

II. PLAN

► **Recognize Your Patterns** Check characteristic, habitual styles you've developed over the years for handling disagreement.

► **Minimize Pitfalls** To choose appropriate strategic approaches, guard against being rigid, irresolute, intrusive or aloof.

III. PREPARE

► **Problem-Solve** Use the preceding steps as a framework to refine your diagnosis and more sharply focus your strategic approach.

► **Practice** When time permits, rehearse approaches unfamiliar to you either mentally, or with friends willing to give you candid feedback

IV. IMPLEMENT

► **Carry Out Your Plan** Consider where (the physical site) to resolve the disagreement and anticipate the emotional atmosphere, skill level and compatibility of the disputants, time constraints, and need for documentation.

► **Evaluate Outcomes** Determine how effectively the disagreement was resolved, using technical, economic, social-psychological, ethical-legal and political evaluation criteria.

► **Follow-up and Learn** Monitor results and consider future monitoring. Where the agreement meets mutual objectives reinforce it. Otherwise, make needed corrections.

REFLECTION

Dealing constructively with disagreement has profound impact. We open ourselves to making real contact with others. We complete unfinished business. Our vision of what's possible expands.

Every human being, like every snowflake, is unique. Disagreement reflects that uniqueness. When we are able to do something constructive with our differences, we move closer to the ideal of one human family living together in a peaceful, productive, and satisfying world.

NOTES

NOTES

NOTES

NOTES

NOW AVAILABLE FROM
CRISP PUBLICATIONS

Books • Videos • CD-ROMs • Computer-Based Training Products

If you enjoyed this book, we have great news for you. There are over 200 books available in the *50-Minute*™ Series. To request a free full-line catalog, contact your local distributor or Crisp Publications, Inc., 1200 Hamilton Court, Menlo Park, CA 94025. Our toll-free number is 800-442-7477. Visit our website at: http://www.crisp-pub.com.

Subject Areas Include:

Management
Human Resources
Communication Skills
Personal Development
Marketing/Sales
Organizational Development
Customer Service/Quality
Computer Skills
Small Business and Entrepreneurship
Adult Literacy and Learning
Life Planning and Retirement

CRISP WORLDWIDE DISTRIBUTION

English language books are distributed worldwide. Major international distributors include:

ASIA/PACIFIC

Australia/New Zealand: In Learning, PO Box 1051, Springwood QLD, Brisbane, Australia 4127   Tel: 61-7-3-841-2286, Facsimile: 61-7-3-841-1580
ATTN: Messrs. Gordon

Philippines: Management Review Publishing, Inc., 301 Tito Jovey Center, Buencamino Str., Alabang, Muntinlupa, Metro Manila, Philippines   Tel: 632-842-3092,
E-mail: robert@easy.net.ph
ATTN: Mr. Trevor Roberts

Japan: Phoenix Associates Co., LTD., Mizuho Bldng, 3-F, 2-12-2, Kami Osaki, Shinagawa-Ku, Tokyo 141   Tel: 81-33-443-7231, Facsimile: 81-33-443-7640
ATTN: Mr. Peter Owans

CANADA

Reid Publishing, Ltd., Box 69559, 60 Briarwood Avenue, Port Credit, Ontario, Canada L5G 3N6   Tel: (905) 842-4428, Facsimile: (905) 842-9327
ATTN: Mr. Steve Connolly/Mr. Jerry McNabb

Trade Book Stores: Raincoast Books, 8680 Cambie Street, Vancouver, B.C., V6P 6M9
Tel: (604) 323-7100, Facsimile: (604) 323-2600
ATTN: Order Desk

EUROPEAN UNION

England: Flex Training, Ltd., 9-15 Hitchin Street, Baldock, Hertfordshire, SG7 6A, England   Tel: 44-1-46-289-6000, Facsimile: 44-1-46-289-2417
ATTN: M. David Willetts

INDIA

Multi-Media HRD, Pvt., Ltd., National House, Tulloch Road, Appolo Bunder, Bombay, India 400-039   Tel: 91-22-204-2281, Facsimile: 91-22-283-6478
ATTN: Messrs. Aggarwal

SOUTH AMERICA

Mexico: Grupo Editorial Iberoamerica, Nebraska 199, Col. Napoles, 03810 Mexico, D.F.
Tel: 525-523-0994, Facsimile: 525-543-1173
ATTN: Señor Nicholas Grepe

SOUTH AFRICA

Alternative Books, PO Box 1345, Ferndale 2160, South Africa
Tel: 27-11-792-7730, Facsimile: 27-11-792-7787
ATTN: Mr. Vernon de Haas